RYAN KORBAN

RYAN KORBAN

interiors

RIZZOLI
NEW YORK

New York · Paris · London · Milan

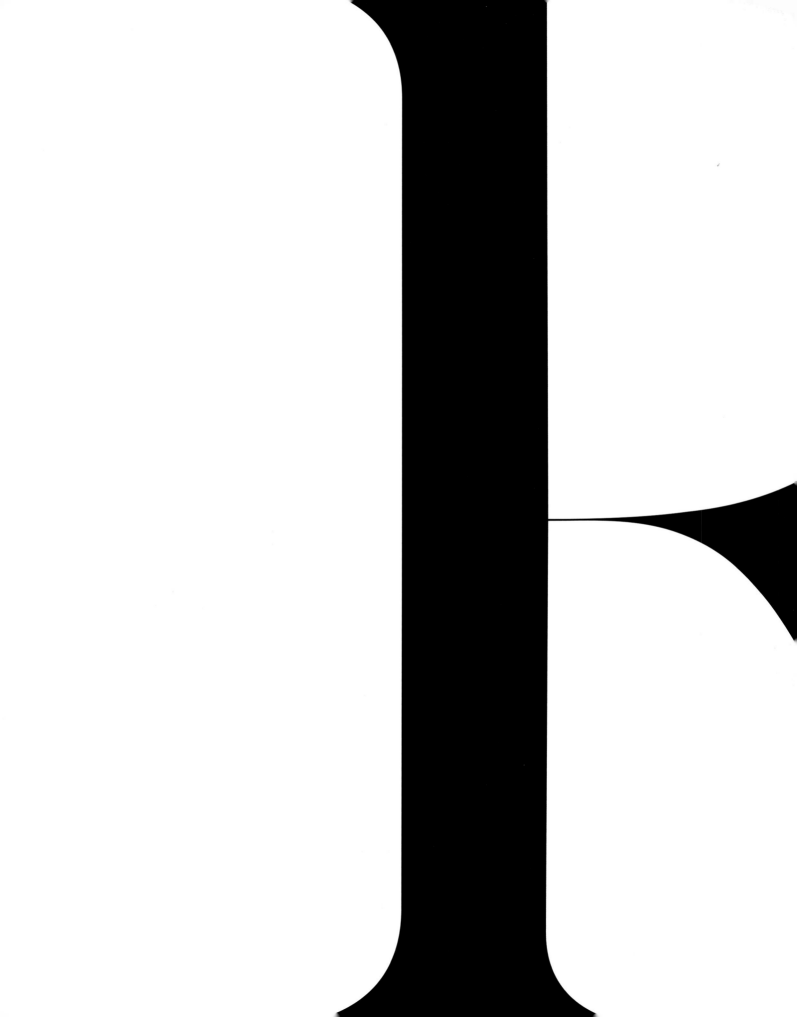

Contents

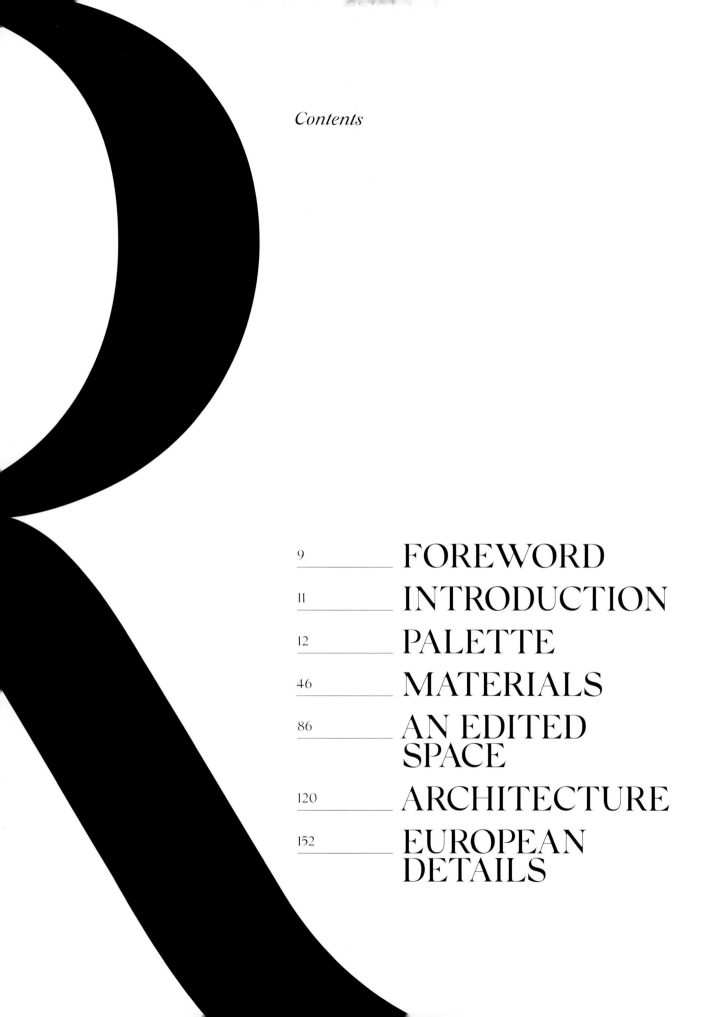

9	FOREWORD
11	INTRODUCTION
12	PALETTE
46	MATERIALS
86	AN EDITED SPACE
120	ARCHITECTURE
152	EUROPEAN DETAILS

"Learn the rules like a pro, so you can break them like an artist." — PABLO PICASSO

FOREWORD

I distinctly recall the first time I saw Ryan Korban's work. It was just over a decade ago at the jam-packed opening of Edon Manor, his defiantly pretty shoe boutique in downtown Manhattan. Ryan was in his early twenties, and his cool-kid crew—a trio of super-chic Traina sisters, designer BFF Alexander Wang, the New York City MOD (models off-duty) squad—was out to support in full force, all partying in head-to-toe black in the petite, incongruously feminine space.

In 2007, the New York retail scene was in a decidedly minimal phase. But with its ultra-femme, Versailles-in-Tribeca-vibe, Edon Manor was unabashedly seductive. Think generously swagged blue satin curtains, pale tufted velvet sofas, enormous statement mirrors, and a lush, towering arrangement of magnolia branches that nearly stretched from one side of the shop to the other. With this romantic space, Ryan not only demonstrated his distinct, devil-may-care point of view, he also immediately established himself as a talented, name-to-know in the design world.

While Ryan's work has since evolved, his essential aesthetic remains the same: opulent yet tailored, with a precisely edited color palette (pink and gray are two of his favorite shades) and hyper-rich materials generously employed to great dramatic effect. Consider the game-changing NYC store he devised for Balenciaga, with its breath-taking acres of green marble and suede, or his boutique for Alexander Wang, with its shockingly sexy fur hammock set against vast expanses of cost-be-damned marble.

Although Ryan admits to being a "sucker" for the eighteenth century (European style in general; French in particular), he is a thoroughly modern creature, totally in his element advising his cadre of clients both young and old on how to harmoniously meld classic with contemporary to create strikingly beautiful spaces.

— AMY ASTLEY, editor in chief of *Architectural Digest*

INTRO–
DUCTION

I'm just going to come out and say it: that notion of the interior decorator with a
board full of coordinated fabric swatches simply isn't relevant anymore. At least not
to today's generation. Young people still appreciate good design—perhaps more than
ever, given their abundant access to information—but they don't want to live in such
a formal way. What they want is an experience.

That's what brands these days are scrounging to offer. They wonder why their
products aren't selling, and it's because they're not generating the kind of interesting
or exciting involvement that draws people to them. When I sit down with a client,
it's the mood or the feeling of the space that's important to them. They don't realize
that's what they're trying to articulate, but it is. Because when I show them a piece of
furniture, it's not enough for them to respond to.

This sort of thinking is the foundation for all of my projects—whether it be a house
or a store or a showroom. For me, it's all about creating a compelling environment.
Things aren't so clearly defined anymore. Stores look like apartments, apartments
look like showrooms. You walk into a new boutique hotel, and it looks like someone's
home. There's a real sense of freedom in design right now—and experimentation.
And perhaps it's a result of having no formal training in this industry, but I naturally
think without constraint—albeit, not always successfully. Yet whether it's through color
palette, materials, architecture, or mood, I'm always trying to push things beyond the
norm. Can I turn that flat ceiling into a curved one? Can I swathe this whole space in
pink? Can we carve a couch out of marble? It's important to look at things in a new way.

That said, I love classical design. I'm a sucker for eighteenth-century-looking
sculpture; obsessed with Versailles. And yet I'm also drawn to twentieth-century
design—I adore the work of Andrée Putman and Mies van der Rohe. What feels interesting and exciting and progressive now is recontextualizing it all—taking pieces out
of their traditional settings and mixing them with contrasting elements. That, to me,
is the essence of contemporary interior design. This book features an array of recent
projects, from uptown townhouses to boutiques downtown. But I approached each
one from the same standpoint: what can I do to create a truly captivating space that
no one ever wants to leave?

— RYAN KORBAN

Part One

PALETTE

From the beginning of my career, I've always been instinctively drawn to color of a more subtle tone. I just didn't connect well with anything bright. Gray has long been my go-to. I call it the new neutral. People usually look to beige or ivory, but for me it's all about gray. Sometimes it's a more blueish cast, other times more taupe. It just looks especially strong with the kinds of materials I like, and it works well with color, which I actually really enjoy using now.

I remember it was seeing a vase full of pink peonies that first turned me onto color. Since then I've loved pale, dusty pink. People respond well to it—and not just millennials! It's a positive hue, and it looks stunning with black and white, which comprises so much of what I do.

The thing about color, though, is that it has to feel tangible. You can give me a Pantone book, and it does nothing for me. It's just too flat. Rather, it will be, say, a swatch of sorbet silk moiré, or a piece of marble in a rich green that sets me off—then I can immediately imagine color in a space.

I try to use color so it's not looked at as color. Which is to say, I deep dive into it so it becomes almost a neutral. The notion of a "pop of color" doesn't work for me. If you want color, use it to excess. Drench the walls in it. Upholster the furniture in varying shades. That's what I did for the Balenciaga stores in New York. We used green everywhere—green marble, green suede—and that stunning emerald became a signature. The same goes for someone's home. It's not simply about slapping on some paint, but rather finding interesting, tactile ways to incorporate color.

Opposite and following pages AQUAZZURA BOUTIQUE, New York

I like color to feel alive—perhaps that's why I'm drawn to floral pinks. They always look good, and work well with my more signature black-and-white palette. For this boutique, pink marble, blush suede, and black-and-white Florentine stripes combine to create a strikingly maximalist space.

Opposite, above, and following pages PRIVATE RESIDENCE, East Sixty-First Street, New York

When it comes to a neutral wall paint, most people automatically go to beige or ivory. I prefer gray. I call it the "new neutral." It leans both masculine and feminine, and, to me, just looks more modern. And it's the perfect canvas on which to build a color story because it works with everything.

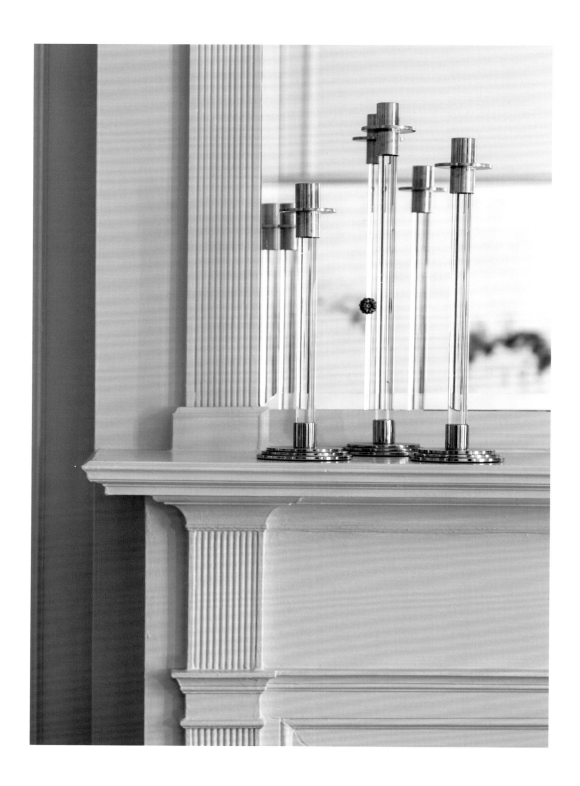

Opposite and following pages FIVESTORY BOUTIQUE, New York
Above A PAIR OF WROUGHT-IRON DOORS, New York

I never approach a room wanting it to be colorful. Rather, the decision is always led by materials or furniture that I find. An Oriental vase was the starting point for the green and mauve color palette, which feels fresh and sleek when paired with black and gold.

Above, opposite, and following pages FIVESTORY BOUTIQUE, New York

This boutique is very black and white, which I love. For its new shoe salon, I didn't set out to do colored walls.
But I found this modern-looking silk moiré wallpaper in light sorbet and thought it would be a beautiful complement
to the graphic look.

"COLOR HAS

HAS

TO FEEL
TANGIBLE."

Previous pages, above, and opposite PRIVATE RESIDENCE, Fifth Avenue, New York

Inspired by the work of Claude Monet, this apartment is awash in watercolor hues—mauve, pale green, ice blue.

Opposite and following pages PRIVATE RESIDENCE, Fifth Avenue, New York
The soft, feminine palette is balanced out by modern, clean-lined furniture.

"I TRY TO USE COLOR SO IT'S NOT LOOKED AT AS COLOR.

I DEEP DIVE INTO IT SO IT BECOMES ALMOST A NEUTRAL."

Opposite THE FRICK COLLECTION, New York
Above PRIVATE RESIDENCE, Fifth Avenue, New York

There's a compelling dichotomy between a polished terrace and its urban backdrop.

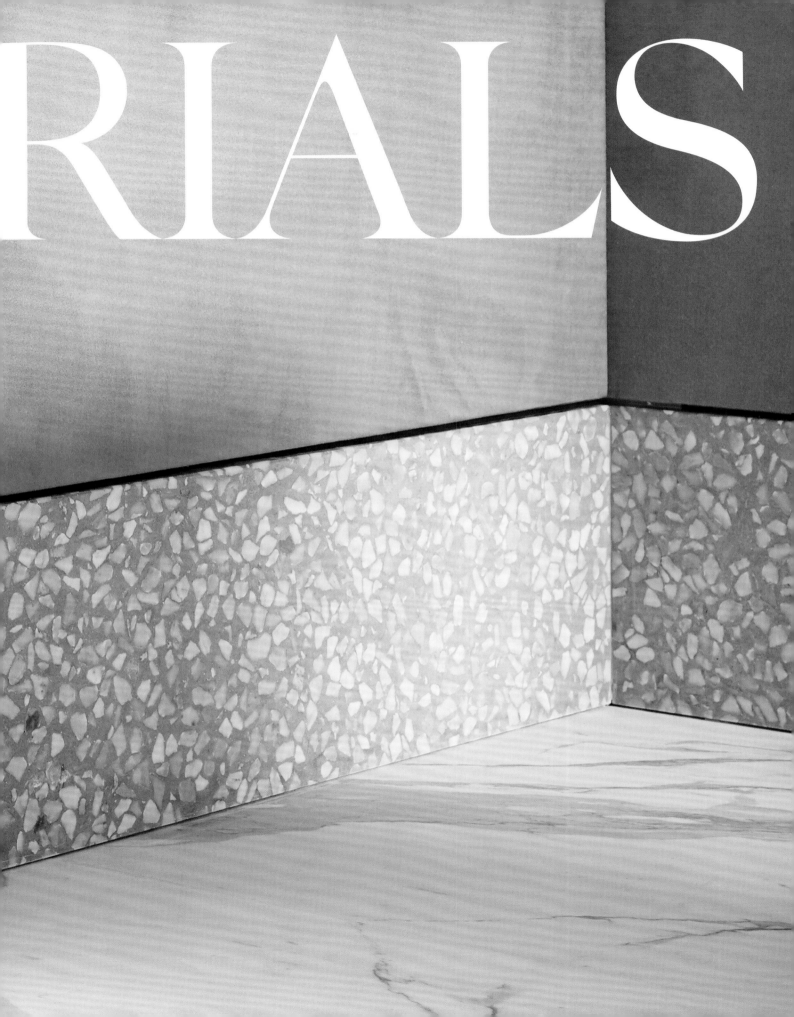

Part Two
MATERIALS

Stone, marble, stainless steel, cerused oak, shagreen . . . Material is the most important thing to me. It inspires everything I do. It's how each project begins: I find the material, and then think of ways to use it.

I love discovering new materials to work with, and exploring new ways to play with the ones that I regularly use. That's what really excites me. How do you clad a ceiling in polished stainless steel? How do you crack resin? How do you rough-surface limestone to make it look like it's just been chipped out of a block? I try things and it doesn't work, but that's part of the process. You get it to work.

Lately I've been interested in using less luxurious materials. As retail continues to change, clients want to do something that's less permanent, or easy to pick up and move. They want transitional spaces. So I've been looking at a lot of industrial materials that people don't usually consider, like acoustic materials that insulate ceilings and walls. Or the mesh metal that companies put on conveyor belts. What if you turned it into curtains? Or used it as a wall treatment? They're interesting challenges. And if you then pair those raw, mechanical materials with suede and chrome, the effect is really cool. Of course, it's harder to experiment with materials in people's homes, because at the end of day, clients just want things to look nice and pretty. But I've found that young people are more willing to push things. Nine out of ten times, if you show them a new way to do something, they respond in a positive way.

Opposite and following pages 40 BLEECKER STREET, New York

Finding new ways to use materials is the most exciting aspect of my job. I love discovering new materials, as well as experimenting with more familiar ones. This residential project was a study in pushing materials to their furthest potential.

Opposite 40 BLEECKER STREET, New York

Here, a polished bronze console table by Eric Schmitt.

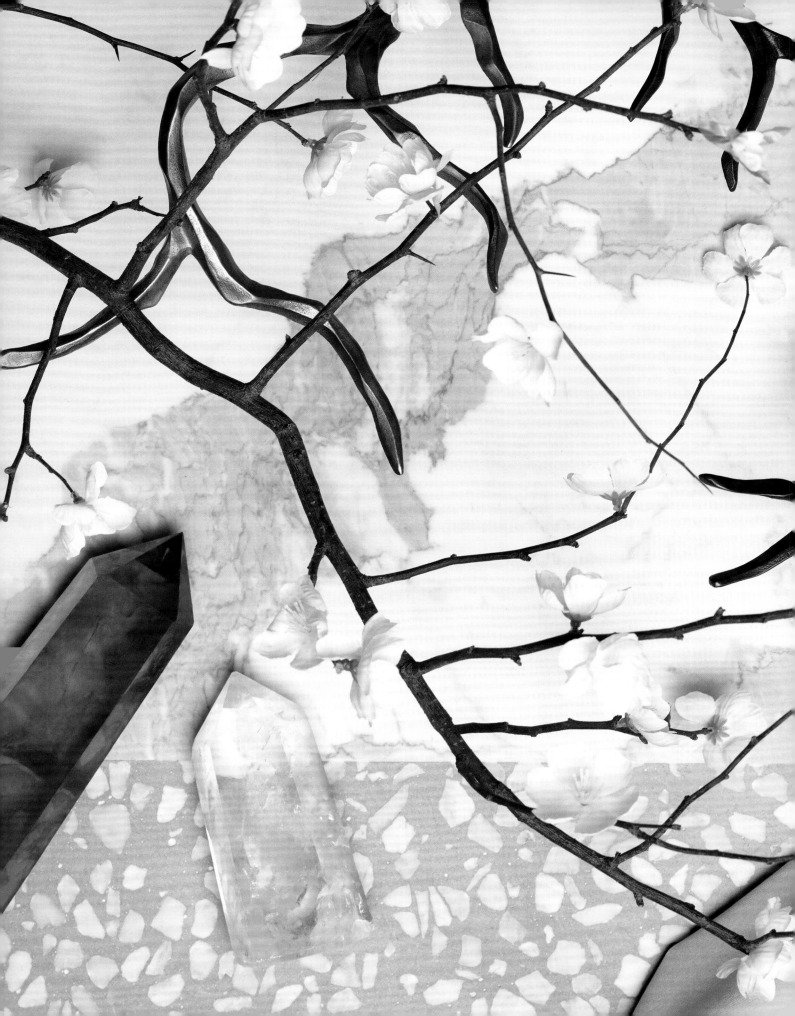

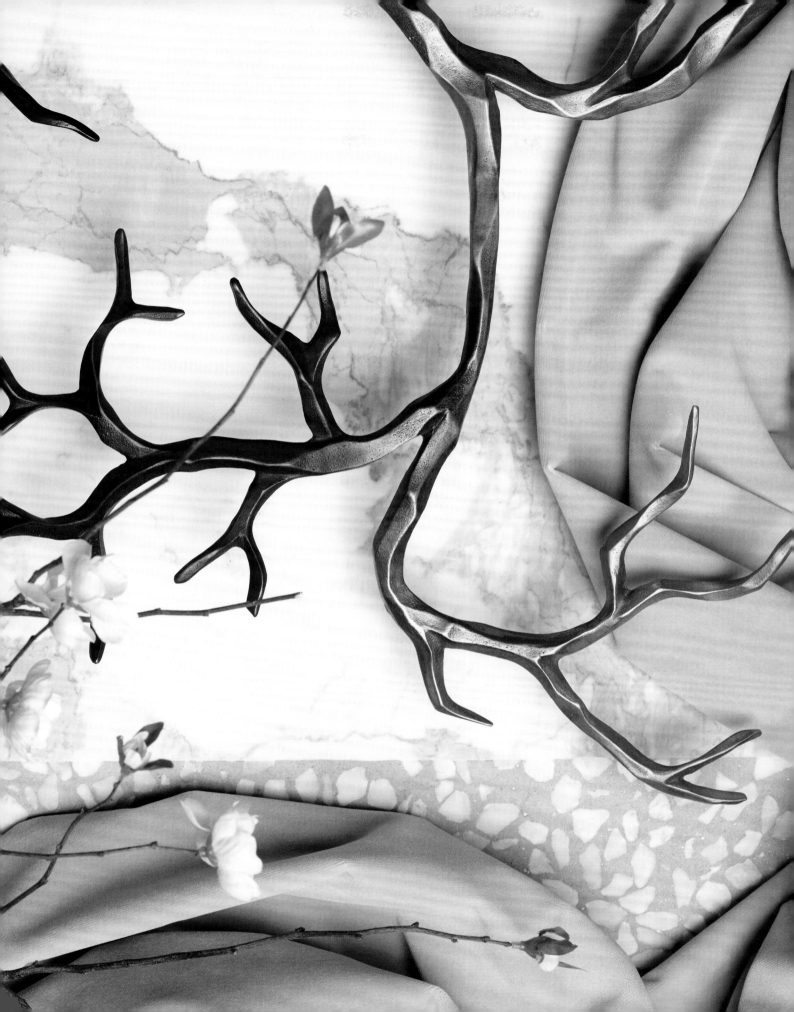

Opposite, above, and following pages 40 BLEECKER STREET, New York

Marble, a favorite material, is reimagined by way of exaggerated proportions and novel forms.

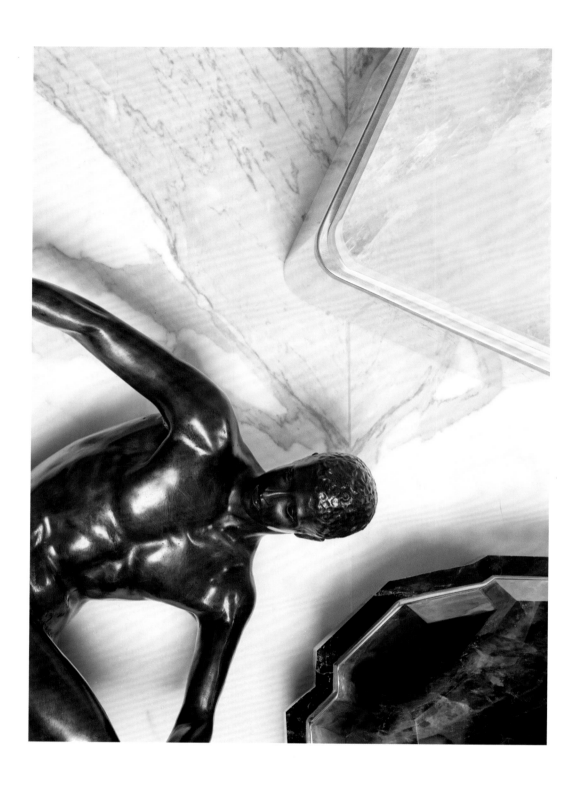

Opposite and above 40 BLEECKER STREET, New York

Cerused oak and marble make for a sleek, yet warm, bathroom.

Above, opposite, and following pages 40 BLEECKER STREET, New York

Using extraordinary materials, like marble, for everyday objects, such as sofas,
is a challenge that more often than not pays off.

Previous pages, above, opposite, and following pages BALENCIAGA BOUTIQUE, New York

Cracked resin is heavy and difficult to use, which is why it feels so unique.
Here, it's molded into a handrail and mounted on mirror for a broken ice effect.

"IT'S HOW EACH PROJECT BEGINS:

I FIND THE MATERIAL, AND THEN THINK OF WAYS TO USE IT."

Opposite, above, and following pages PRIVATE RESIDENCE, Seventy-Second Street, New York

Plush velvets and raw silk lend a cool, masculine allure to this apartment.

Opposite, above, and following pages PRIVATE RESIDENCE, Seventy-Second Street, New York

Suede walls and silk carpeting create a sense of warmth and intimacy in the bedroom—it begs you to be barefoot in it.

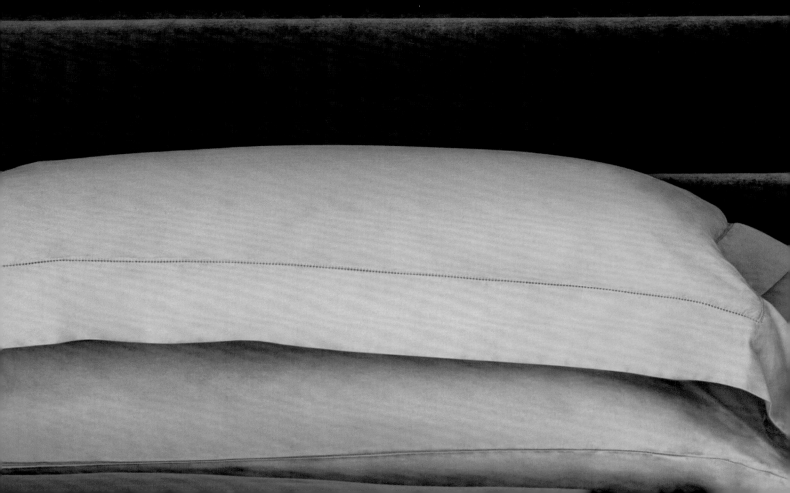

Part Three

AN EDITED SPACE

I started out my career with a more-is-more approach to design, and I still have a fondness for it. My all-time favorite example is Yves Saint Laurent's apartment on rue de Babylone in Paris. That dense, eclectic mix of different eras and cultures takes on its own style and can be very cool and interesting. But I've found, in the end, that you get a little tired of it. On the flip side, that very minimal look with nothing but a few mid-century pieces feels outdated to me. What feels fresh and new is a perfectly edited room—one stripped of all but a few really strong, special items. It's harder to do right—it takes time and experience to understand what are the most important things to have in a space, and to be able to strike a harmonious balance between them all. But the result is so chic.

I liken decorating a room to getting dressed. You need to try a couple things on, change your shoes. You can't just buy a few pieces from a furniture showroom and expect them all to work together. You have to bring in a ton of stuff and then edit it down from there.

Of course, there are a few basic elements that I always incorporate, like lighting. I'm always gravitating towards sculptural lamps, whether they're standing or ceiling ones. Real showstoppers. It's like picking out art for me. And you'd be hard-pressed to find a space that I've designed that doesn't have plaster or bronze sculptures in it. A handful of mirrors, too. The ultimate goal is to evoke a sense of culture and travel and lives well lived, in a perfectly curated manner.

Opposite, page 91, and pages 92–93 PRIVATE RESIDENCE, Park Avenue, New York

A cleanly designed space calls for ornate wallpaper, like this one from de Gournay.

Above THE STRONG LINES OF THE CITY

Opposite PRIVATE RESIDENCE, Park Avenue, New York

Within a sleek monochromatic apartment, like this one, it's fun to play up a powder room and treat it like a jewel box.
In fact, I often have more fun decorating these little "non-spaces," as I like to call them, than I do living rooms, because you
can really let your imagination run wild.

Page 102, above, and opposite PRIVATE RESIDENCE, Park Avenue, New York

The pared-down aesthetic of the house extends into the stone bathroom, which has minimal fixtures and hardware.

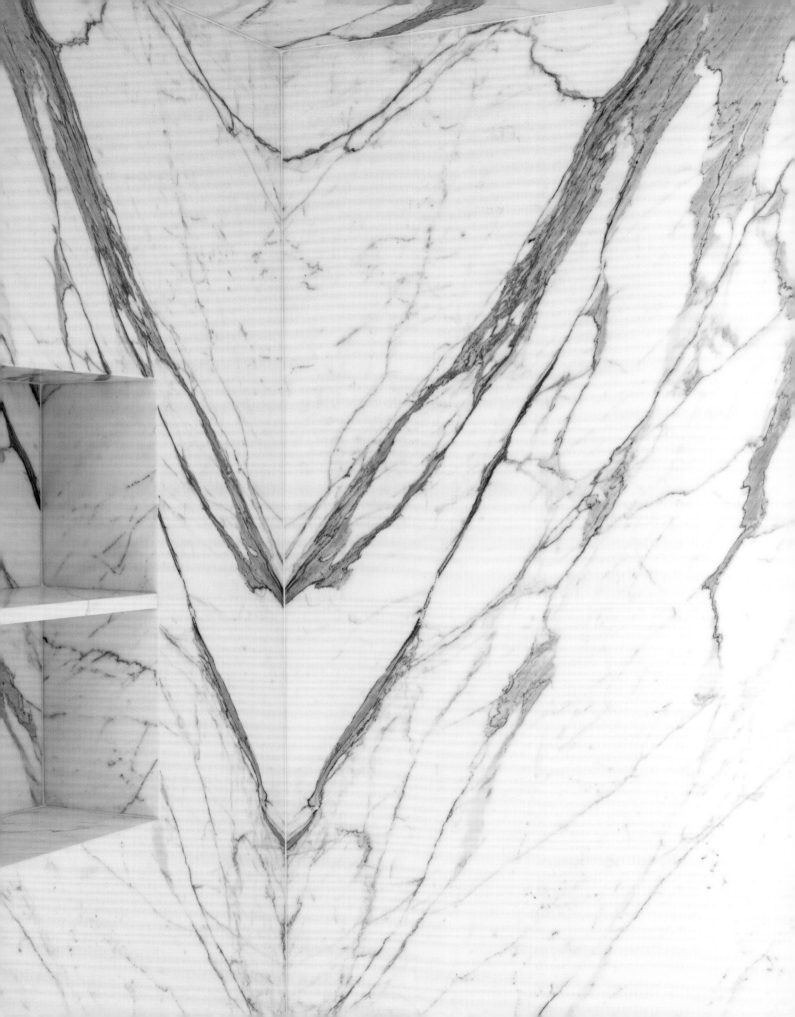

HELMUT NEWTON TASCHEN

Opposite and above PRIVATE RESIDENCE, Park Avenue, New York

This is a playful but edited-down room that a child can grow into.

Opposite PRIVATE RESIDENCE, Madison Avenue, New York

Clean lines and a muted color palette allow the art to be the focus in this apartment.

Opposite PRIVATE RESIDENCE, Madison Avenue, New York

Everything in this apartment has its place, including the bookshelves, which are flush against the wall and wrapped in suede, so they almost disappear.

ARCHIT

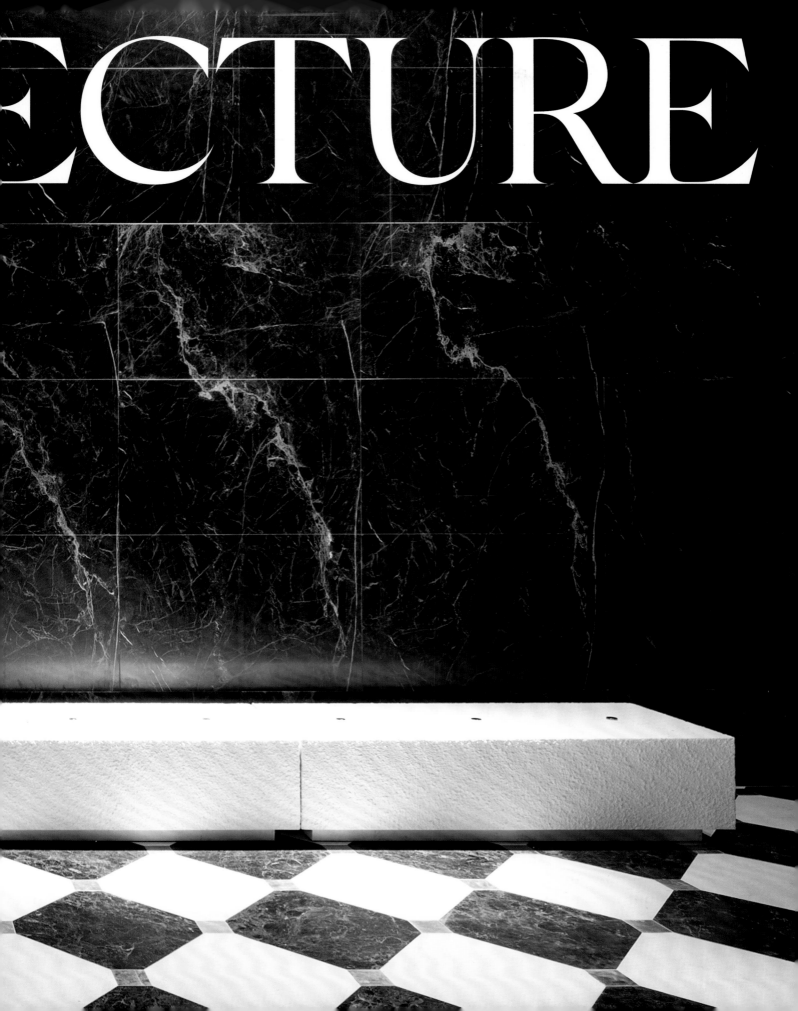

Part Four

ARCHI-TECTURE

In this industry, the closest relationship I have is with my architect. I look at everything through his lens. That's where the magic of design stems from. But unless you're redoing a space from scratch, you have to be realistic about what you're working with. The majority of my projects are in New York City, and clients have these grand ideas, but they have low-ceilinged, boxy parameters. You have to allow the architecture of a space to lead. That's the most important aspect of a successful space. So if you have a box, you need to be open to what style best suits that. Bringing big, ornate furniture into a space with unimpressive ceiling heights and standard windows will actually make the room feel more cramped. But taking a more minimal approach, and using all low-slung furniture with clean lines, will open it up. That's the trick: go low with the furniture and super high with the drapes. And do it all in really luxurious fabrics.

I find my favorite pieces of design are usually created by people with strong architectural backgrounds, like Eileen Gray and Mies van der Rohe. Much of van der Rohe's furniture is based on the notion of cantilever or suspension. It's like a challenge of space. I've been using a lot of his designs lately, but reimagined in different fabrics. You mostly see them in polished stainless steel with black leather. I reupholstered his chairs in sheared gray mink, and all of a sudden they were new again. Andrée Putman wasn't an architect, but she thought like one. She saw space as space. Whether it was the department store Le Bon Marché or the Concorde or someone's home, she approached each project with a radical modernity. And she would often use the same furniture—her own crescent moon designs—for each one. I love that idea of having a signature that looks great everywhere.

Opposite and following pages BALENCIAGA BOUTIQUE, New York

Museums around the world were the inspiration for this space. Its grand proportions allowed for a design that was equally monumental.

"YOU HAVE TO ALLOW

THE ARCHI–TECTURE OF A SPACE TO LEAD."

Opposite and following pages, PRIVATE RESIDENCE, Tenth Avenue, New York

The lines of the building dictated the design of this apartment, which feels very spare yet substantial with its large-scale pieces.

Opposite PRIVATE RESIDENCE, Tenth Avenue, New York

I love the furniture of Mies van der Rohe because the design elements stem from architectural ideas.
For this apartment, I reupholstered his *Brno* chairs in gray sheared mink. All of a sudden they felt new again.

Previous pages, above, and opposite PRIVATE RESIDENCE, Tenth Avenue, New York

The materials used—bronze, plaster, marble—are more associated with architecture than furnishings.

Previous pages, opposite, and above PRIVATE RESIDENCE, Tenth Avenue, New York

There aren't a lot of pieces in this apartment, so each one feels singular, like this Milo Baughman *Wave* chaise.

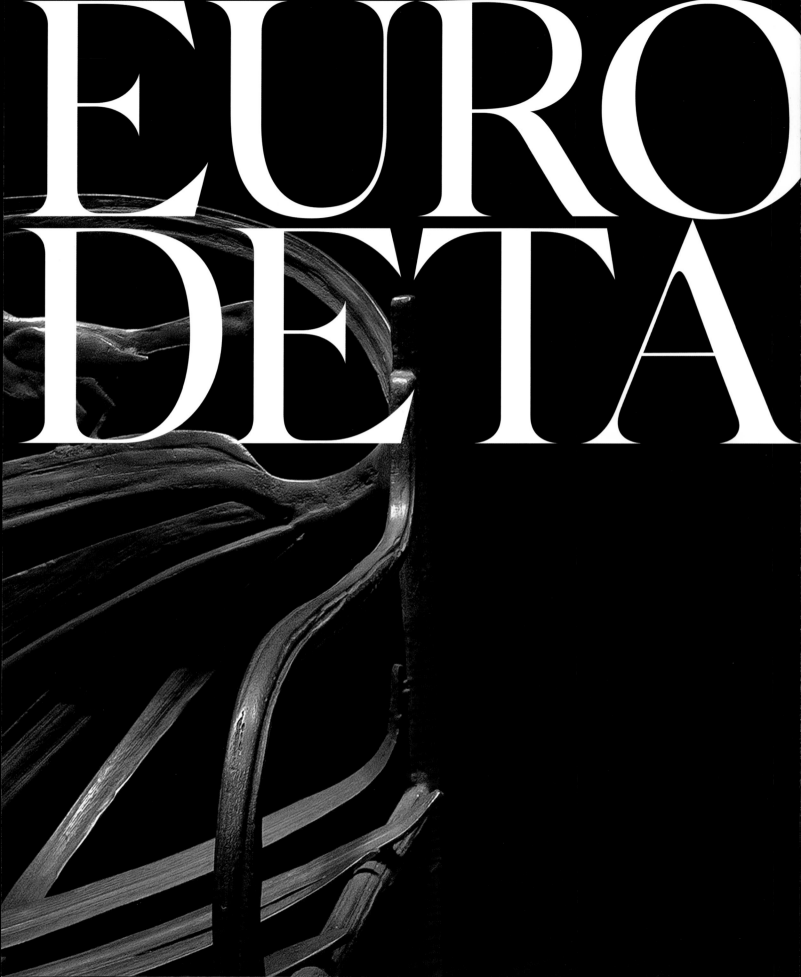

Part Five

EUROPEAN DETAILS

Europe has always been a huge inspiration for me. But as beautiful as it is, it can often be overwhelming, design-wise. You walk into a beautiful room in Paris or Rome, and it takes your breath away. But you can't live like that—it's unattainable. However, you can extract some of the elements. I tend to start from a place of over-the-top European opulence, which I temper with something modern—and that's been my design aesthetic from the beginning. I love using elegant, formal materials in very informal ways. For instance, a silk velvet, which is often seen on settees, done on a sleek sofa. Or an elaborate gold-leaf frame for modern black-and-white photographs. Vice versa, I'm always stripping down old Louis XVI chairs and reupholstering them in suede or leather. It's about reimagining these periodic elements—and reintroducing them.

My younger clients want their homes to feel intrinsically unique. They don't want a cookie cutter apartment. Social media has a lot to do with that because they're constantly sharing images of their personal space. Yet they don't want their homes looking like those of their grandparents—and that's usually the comment I hear when I bring them to antique showrooms. But when you pull out a pair of French antique chairs and recontextualize them beside a modern cocktail table, the response is overwhelmingly positive. It feels curated in a fresh, new way.

Opposite and following pages SOTHEBY'S DESIGNER SHOWHOUSE, New York, 2014

For this room, I imagined that someone won the lottery and went shopping at Sotheby's. It was intended to be over-the-top. An exaggerated and playful mix of pieces and time periods make for a fantastical space.

"I START FROM
A PLACE OF
OVER-THE-TOP
EUROPEAN
OPULENCE.

WHICH I TEMPER
WITH SOMETHING
MODERN."

Above and following pages SOTHEBY'S DESIGNER SHOWHOUSE, New York, 2014

Despite being filled with antiques, such as a Louis XV japanned commode and Louis XVI giltwood marquise chairs, the room has a modern feel—a result of the mix of pieces and the graphic color palette.

Page 162, opposite, above, and following pages AQUAZZURA BOUTIQUE, New York

Florentine churches were the inspiration for this shoe store. The architecture and striking marble patterns were reimagined in a modern way.

"IT'S ABOUT REIMAGINING THESE PERIODIC

ELEMENTS—AND REINTRODUCING THEM."

Opposite and above AQUAZZURA BOUTIQUE, New York

While the foundation appears old and European, the furniture is more contemporary and sexy. The brass-and-marble tables were made by Gabriel Scott to resemble spiked high heels.

VERUSCHK

Previous pages, above, and opposite PRIVATE RESIDENCE, Sixty-First Street, New York

With its moldings, brass fixtures, and black-and-white marble floors, this Manhattan townhouse has a stately English feel.

Opposite PRIVATE RESIDENCE, Sixty-First Street, New York

The idea was to contrast the elegant European feel of the apartment with modern, almost brutalist lighting and furniture.

Above and opposite PRIVATE RESIDENCE, Sixty-First Street, New York

JoAnn Patterson's organic sculptures beautifully temper a sleek space.

"I LOVE USING ELEGANT, FORMAL

MATERIALS IN INFORMAL WAYS."

Previous pages, opposite, and above PRIVATE RESIDENCE, Sixty-First Street, New York

Regency-inspired dining chairs are reimagined with a contemporary fabric from Dedar.

Above and opposite PRIVATE RESIDENCE, Sixty-First Street, New York

I love how in mixing pieces from different periods, like this gilt rococo mirror with an Italian credenza from the 1970s, you create a world of your own.

Above PRIVATE RESIDENCE, Sixty-First Street, New York

A slice of Europe hidden in the back courtyard.

ACKNOWLEDGMENTS

I'd like to extend my deepest gratitude to the following people:

Karin Nelson
Amy Astley
Charles Miers
Anthony Petrillose
Victorine Lamothe
Jacob Wildschiodtz
Elina Asanti
Nicole Irizarry
Stefanie Brückler
Kari Stuart
Björn Wallander
Naho Kubota
Gieves Anderson
Brittany Ambridge
Anthony Cotsifas
Hugh Lippe
Dean Kaufman
Phoenix Gallery
Alan Chan
Alexandra Niacato
Paul Bennett—*thank you for bringing my designs to life.*
Lisa Wright
Yuliette Rodriguez
Kevin Law
Donald Brown
Bill Schwinghammer
David Codikow
Raymond Chalme and everyone at Broad Street Development
Dani Ganis and everyone at Douglas Elliman
Kate Lee
Michael King
Courtney Dolan
Alexander Wang
Fred and Claire Distenfeld
Mario Dedivanovic
And a special thanks to Fran Parente

PHOTOGRAPHY CREDITS

Ryan Korban: Interiors

First published in the United States of America in 2018
by Rizzoli International Publications Inc.
300 Park Avenue South, New York, NY 10010
www.rizzoliusa.com

FOREWORD BY Amy Astley
EDITED BY Karin Nelson

PUBLISHER: Charles Miers
ASSOCIATE PUBLISHER: Anthony Petrillose
EDITOR: Victorine Lamothe
PRODUCTION MANAGER: Barbara Sadick
DESIGN COORDINATOR: Kayleigh Jankowski

ART DIRECTION AND DESIGN BY NR2154
Jacob Wildschiødtz, Elina Asanti, Nicole Irizarry, Stefanie Brückler

Distributed in the U.S. trade by Random House, New York

ISBN: 978-0-8478-6142-2
Library of Congress Control Number: 2018939224

2018 2019 2020 2021 / 10 9 8 7 6 5 4 3 2 1

Printed in China